ANTON EDELMANN'S
MUSIC & MENUS FOR ROMANCE

ANTON EDELMANN'S
MUSIC & MENUS FOR ROMANCE

INSPIRING ROMANTIC MUSIC

SENSUOUS TEMPTING RECIPES

PAVILION

First published in Great Britain in 1999 by
PAVILION BOOKS LIMITED
London House, Great Eastern Wharf
Parkgate Road, London SW11 4NQ

Text © Anton Edelmann 1999
Photographs © Laurie Evans 1999
Food Stylist: Maxine Clark Props Stylist: Lesley Richardson
For picture credits see page 88
Design and layout © Pavilion Books Ltd. 1999

Designed by David Fordham

A CIP catalogue record for this book is available
from the British Library.

ISBN 1 85793 997 2

Set in Galliard by MATS, Southend-on-Sea, Essex
Printed in China by Imago

2 4 6 8 10 9 7 5 3 1

This book can be ordered direct from the publisher. Please contact
the Marketing Department. But try your bookshop first.

Frontispiece: Skewers of Tiger Prawns in Smoked Bacon Caribbean-style (see page 47)

Acknowledgements

Nothing good is ever achieved without enthusiasm, and for showing this essential quality in abundance, and for their dedication and hard work, I thank all my colleagues and friends who helped with this book. My special thanks to the General Manager of The Savoy, Michael Shepherd, for his generosity, and to Derek Rooke, Nancy Kinchella, Peter Woods, Ramon Pajares, Sandrine Solans and all the others who gave so freely of their time and showed so much patience and goodwill. Last, but not least, thanks to my wife, Sue, for her constant encouragement in all I do.

Contents

Romantic Classics

ROMANTIC MENU 1
Frédéric CHOPIN
Nocturne No. 1 in B Flat Minor 5.56
Vitalij Margolis (piano)

ROMANTIC MENU 2
Ludwig van BEETHOVEN
Sonata for Piano No. 14 in C Sharp Minor Op. 27/2
'Moonlight Sonata' 6.01
Dubravka Tomsic (piano)

ROMANTIC MENU 3
Joseph HAYDN
Extract from Quartet for Strings in C Major
'Emperor' Op. 76/3 1.46
Caspar da Salò Quartet

ROMANTIC MENU 4
Johannes BRAHMS
Waltz in A Flat Major Op. 39 1.25
Dieter Goldman (piano)

ROMANTIC MENU 5
Robert SCHUMANN
Träumerei Op. 15 No. 7 (Dreaming) 2.39
Dieter Goldman (piano)

ROMANTIC MENU 6
Antonio VIVALDI
Concerto for Mandolin and Orchestra
in C Major RV 425 3.11
Eugen Duvier, Camerata Romana

ROMANTIC MENU 7
Felix MENDELSSOHN-BARTHOLDY
A Midsummer Night's Dream 6.37
Alberto Lizzio, Philharmonia Slavonica

ROMANTIC MENU 8
Franz SCHUBERT
Quintet for Piano in A Major 'Trout'
Op. 114 D667 6.58
Caspar da Salò Quartet

Romantic Classics

ROMANTIC MENU 9
GUSTAV MAHLER
EXTRACT FROM SYMPHONY NO. 5
IN C SHARP MINOR 3.55
ANTON NANUT, RADIO SYMPHONY ORCHESTRA LJUBLIJANA

ROMANTIC MENU 10
JOHANN SEBASTIAN BACH
AIR ON A G STRING 5.48
FRANK SHIPWAY, ROYAL PHILHARMONIC ORCHESTRA

ROMANTIC MENU 11
CLAUDE DEBUSSY
SUITE BERGAMASQUE - CLAIR DE LUNE 5.19
DIETER GOLDMAN (PIANO)

ROMANTIC MENU 12
WOLFGANG AMADEUS MOZART
SERENADE NO. 13 IN G MAJOR 'EINE KLEINE NACHTMUSIK' KV
525 6.43
ALFRED SCHOLZ, CAMERATA SLAVONICA

ROMANTIC MENU 13
ANTONIN DVORÁK
SERENADE FOR STRINGS IN E MAJOR OP. 22 6.00
EUGEN DUVIER, CAMERATA ROMANA

ROMANTIC MENU 14
GIACCOMO PUCCINI
LA BOHÈME 'CHE GELIDA MANINA' 3.53
HANSPETER GMÜR, NUREMBERG SYMPHONY ORCHESTRA

ROMANTIC MENU 15
PYOTR I. TCHAIKOVSKY
EXTRACT FROM ROMEO AND JULIET FANTASY OVERTURE 6.09
LAWRENCE SIEGEL, NEW PHILHARMONIA ORCHESTRA LONDON

Opposite: Banana and Ginger Souffle with Passion Fruit Sauce

Introduction

I SEE FOOD AND MUSIC as two of the threads that bind us to each other and to the past. We owe a great deal to this tradition, particularly in a world that is growing ever more complex, and where the path of change seems to quicken and time is becoming a scarce and precious commodity. This book is about using these two threads to the best possible advantage and also about adding immense pleasure to your life by taking delight in simple things that are readily available. I hope here to inspire you and encourage you on to ever greater culinary achievements.

All through the ages the appreciation of music and the skill of cooking were both considered as art, and they had an aura of mystery about them. Nowadays the first depends mainly on your own personal taste and the size of your CD collection, and not necessarily on your own performance on the piano or violin. Cooking, on the other hand, is, of course, all about personal performance. Unfortunately, it is still very often portrayed as something difficult and complicated – an art form demanding special skills or a science full of secrets known only to a chosen few.

Let us therefore begin by setting this right: cooking is simply the preparation of carefully measured ingredients, mixing them together and then, if necessary, heating them for the correct amount of time at the right temperature. Of course, as with a romantic relationship, there has to be a certain chemistry to make a dish really special.

To achieve harmony between food, music and romance, an intricate and well-thought-out balance and blending of flavours, textures, melodies and surroundings have to be struck to satisfy our senses, desires and expectations. The occasion defines the style from the outset and the secret lies in the planning. Is it a formal engagement, a candlelit dinner, a stormy and steamy affair? Menus must be structured carefully around the occasion, taking into consideration the time of day as well, and the desired effect.

It is important to remember that late at night is not a suitable time for a long and heavy dinner which could end up giving you indigestion or, indeed, stop you from sleeping. At the other end of the scale, a meal in the middle of the day should contain dishes to keep your energy levels high. The choice of ingredients – and this includes the music – is therefore of paramount importance.

The rule is keep it simple. For the food, always look for fresh produce, free of additives, and try to use seasonal ingredients – this will bring variety and health to your diet too. Never attempt the impossible. Always choose dishes that you have cooked before and feel confident with, and remember that practice makes perfect. The more you cook, the more skilled and adventurous you will become.

As for the music, each piece should flow harmoniously with each course – something tantalising and light with lots of spirit to start with, followed perhaps by more intensity to help break down any barriers and to allow for deeper soul-searching. Music for the dessert can then be good-humoured, even frivolous and teasing, which will help to create the magical effect you are both looking for.

True success, of course, requires more than just the right music or the right food. The whole experience is an expression and reflection of your personality. Everyone has their own philosophy and their own approach, so do not be afraid to break the rules. The whole experience should be a pleasure – the creation of the food in your kitchen, the selection of the music and the wines, and then sitting down in the company of the one you love, to eat, listen and enjoy the fruits of your labours.

Formal Engagement Supper

ACERTAIN ETIQUETTE SHOULD BE OBSERVED FOR THIS MEAL, BUT THAT DOES NOT MEAN BORING OR UNIMAGINATIVE FOOD – AFTER ALL, THERE IS PROBABLY SOMEONE PRESENT WHOM YOU WOULD LIKE TO IMPRESS. WHAT WE ARE LOOKING FOR IN THE MEAL, AS IN THE RELATIONSHIP, IS FLAVOUR AND DEPTH. THIS WE HAVE IN ABUNDANCE IN THE FORMAL ENGAGEMENT SUPPER MENU.

THE TART, WITH ITS SWEET TOMATOES, RICH AND COMFORTING MOZZARELLA AND PUNGENT MARJORAM, MELTS INTO A TRULY WONDERFUL EATING EXPERIENCE. IF YOU SHOULD HAVE A LITTLE TRUFFLE OIL IN YOUR FRIDGE, NOW IS THE TIME TO USE IT.

THE GUINEA FOWL WITH A HERB AND ROASTED GARLIC CRUST WORKS SO HARMONIOUSLY WITH THE FRESHNESS OF THE MINTED PEA PURÉE. A WONDERFUL SURPRISE!

ROASTED PINEAPPLE IS A CLASSIC DISH, AND I AM SURE THAT IT WILL CONVINCE EVEN THE MOST DIFFICULT PROSPECTIVE MOTHER-IN-LAW OF YOUR HONOURABLE INTENTIONS.

CHERRY TOMATO TART
— WITH —
MARJORAM

Serves 6

450g/15¾oz puff pastry
1½ egg white
24 cherry tomatoes, cut in half
450g/15¾oz mozzarella cheese (preferably buffalo
mozzarella), cut into 6mm/¼in slices
¾ bunch fresh marjoram
juice of 1¾ lemon
6 tbsp olive oil
3 handfuls rocket/arugula
truffle oil (optional)
salt and freshly ground pepper

Heat the oven to 200°C/400°F/Gas Mark 6.

Roll out the puff pastry to 6mm/¼in thickness and cut out 4 discs, each 15cm/6in in diameter. Place the pastry discs on a greased baking sheet and prick each several times with a fork. Brush with the egg white, then chill for about 15 minutes.

Arrange the tomatoes and mozzarella in alternate layers on top of the pastry discs. Season generously with salt and pepper. Bake for 15–20 minutes. Sprinkle the marjoram leaves on top and bake for a further 2–3 minutes.

Mix the lemon juice with the olive oil. Season, and mix with the rocket. Trickle a little truffle oil over each tart, if using. Arrange a little dressed rocket on top, and serve immediately.

Opposite: Cherry Tomato Tart with Marjoram

GRILLED GUINEA FOWL
— WITH —
GARLIC AND HERB CRUST

Serves 6

3 whole garlic bulbs
4½ tbsp olive oil
4½ tbsp chopped fresh herbs (flat-leaf parsley,
tarragon and coriander/cilantro in equal amounts)
6 guinea fowl breasts with the bones left in
1½ onion, peeled and finely chopped
150ml/5¼fl oz dry white wine
150ml/5¼fl oz double cream/heavy cream
750g/25½oz frozen peas
3 tbsp finely chopped fresh mint
3 tsp Dijon mustard
4½ tbsp freshly grated Parmesan cheese
salt and freshly ground pepper

Heat the oven to 220°C/425°F/Gas Mark 7.

Break up the garlic into cloves. Peel and crush 1 clove, and reserve. Place the remaining garlic cloves on a piece of foil, sprinkle with a few drops of olive oil and wrap up into a parcel. Place in the oven and roast for 30 minutes or until the garlic cloves are very soft. Remove the garlic (leave the oven on). Set aside 12 garlic cloves for the garnish. Squeeze out the soft pulp from the skins of the remaining garlic cloves and mix with the chopped herbs.

Heat a ridged cast-iron grill pan. Season the guinea fowl, then turn in a little olive oil to coat lightly. Place on the hot grill pan, skin side down, and sear until marked with charred lines. Transfer the guinea fowl to a roasting pan, skin side up, and place in the oven to roast for about 25 minutes or until just cooked.

Continued on page 15

ROASTED PINEAPPLE
✣ WITH ✣
DARK RUM

Serves 6

195g/6¾oz/15¾ tbsp sugar
1½ tsp peeled and grated fresh ginger
1½ fresh hot red chilli
750 ml/27fl oz water
¾ banana, mashed
75 ml/3fl oz dark rum
2 medium-sized ripe pineapple
9 vanilla pods/vanilla beans,
cut in half lengthways and then across in half

Continued from page 12

In the meantime, heat the remaining olive oil in a saucepan and sweat the onion until soft and translucent. Add the reserved crushed garlic and sweat for a further minute. Add the wine and boil to reduce by two-thirds, then add the cream and reduce by half. Put in the peas and bring back to the boil. Using a hand-held blender, blend the mixture briefly into a rough purée. Add the mint and season well. Keep warm.

Heat the grill/broiler to high.

Remove the bones from the guinea fowl. Brush the skin side of each breast with some of the mustard and top with the garlic pulp and herb mixture. Sprinkle with the grated Parmesan cheese and grill until lightly browned.

Place two spoonfuls of the pea purée on each warmed plate and top with a guinea fowl breast. Garnish with the remaining whole garlic cloves.

Heat the oven to 200°C/400°F/Gas Mark 6.

Place the sugar in a heavy-based saucepan and melt over gentle heat, then cook until amber in colour. Stirring constantly, add the ginger, chilli and water and bring to the boil. Reduce the liquid by half. Add the mashed banana and rum, and stir well. Remove from the heat.

Peel the pineapple using a sharp knife; leave the green crown of leaves on top. With a small knife, make incisions in the flesh and spike evenly with the pieces of vanilla pod. Place the pineapple in an ovenproof dish, standing upright, and pour the rum sauce all over the flesh. Bake for 45 minutes, basting often with the sauce.

Serve the pineapple whole, with the sauce on the side, and ice-cream or a sorbet if you wish.

Opposite: Grilled Guinea Fowl with Garlic and Herb Crust

Romantic Menu 2

Musician's Secret Dream

MUSSELS MAKE A VERY LIGHT YET INTENSELY-FLAVOURED STARTER. HERE THESE STARS OF THE SEA ARE ENHANCED WITH THE STAR ANISE, PERNOD AND FENNEL – A CULINARY ENSEMBLE MADE IN HEAVEN. MUSSELS NEED TO BE COOKED ONLY VERY BRIEFLY, SO THAT THEIR JUICY SOFTNESS IS PRESERVED.

RACK OF LAMB, ON THE OTHER HAND, REQUIRES A LOT OF CARE AND SKILL IN ITS PREPARATION, QUALITIES A MUSICIAN HAS IN ABUNDANCE. IT IS SAID THAT FIGS, NOT APPLES, WERE OFFERED TO ADAM IN THE GARDEN OF EDEN. I CAN WELL BELIEVE THIS, AS THERE ARE FEW THINGS AS BEAUTIFUL TO EAT AS A RIPE AND JUICY FIG. THE SIMPLE COUSCOUS PARTNERING THE FIGS IS FULL OF EXOTIC FLAVOURS – A PERFECT COUNTERPOINT TO THE LAMB.

BY WAY OF CONTRAST, THE TRIFLE OFFERS A COMFORTING FINISH TO THE MEAL, WITH MASCARPONE ACCOMPANIED BY AMARETTO DELIVERING THE ULTIMATE CRESCENDO.

MUSSELS
~ WITH ~
PERNOD, FENNEL AND STAR ANISE

Serves 2

2 tbsp olive oil
½ small onion, peeled and finely chopped
1 garlic clove, peeled and crushed
½ fennel bulb, peeled and finely diced
750g/1lb 10oz fresh mussels, scrubbed and beards removed
150ml/5½fl oz dry white wine
1 star anise
100ml/3½fl oz double cream/heavy cream
1½ tbsp Pernod or Ricard
2 tsp finely chopped fresh flat-leaf parsley
freshly ground pepper

Heat the oil in a large, heavy-based pan, add the onion and sweat until soft and translucent. Add the garlic and sweat for a further minute. Add the fennel, mussels, white wine and star anise. Cover the pan tightly and cook, shaking the pan frequently, until all the mussel shells have opened up (discard any that do not).

Tip into a colander set in a bowl. Cover the mussels in the colander with a damp cloth to keep them moist. Allow the mussel stock in the bowl to rest for a few minutes so that any sand that might have been in the shells can settle on the bottom, then carefully ladle out the stock into the pan. Bring to the boil and reduce by half.

Add the cream to the reduced stock and season with a little black pepper. Stir in the Pernod or Ricard. Return the mussels to the pan and toss in the sauce. Serve immediately, sprinkled with the parsley.

Above: Mussels with Pernod, Fennel and Star Anise

ROASTED RACK OF LAMB
WITH FIGS
— AND —
GREEK YOGHURT SAUCE

Serves 2

1 small best end (rack) of lamb,
weighing about 500g/1lb 2oz, all fat removed
50g/1¾oz/¼ cup 'instant' couscous
50ml/2fl oz orange juice
3 ripe but firm figs, cut into quarters
½ small red onion, peeled and finely chopped
¼ tsp ground cardamom
2 tbsp chopped fresh mint
200ml/7fl oz plain Greek yoghurt/thick plain yoghurt
1 small garlic clove, peeled and crushed
juice of ¼ lemon
1½ tbsp finely grated cucumber
1½ tbsp extra virgin olive oil
salt and freshly ground pepper

Heat the oven to 220°C/425°F/Gas Mark 7.

Season the best end of lamb and put into a roasting pan. Roast for 15–20 minutes (the meat will be pink). Remove and leave to rest in a warm place.

While the lamb is roasting, combine the couscous and orange juice in a small pan and simmer gently until all the liquid has been absorbed, stirring occasionally. Add the figs, onion, cardamom and half the mint, and fold in gently. Remove from the heat and keep warm.

Mix together the yoghurt, garlic, lemon juice, the remaining mint, cucumber and extra virgin olive oil.

Spoon the figs and couscous on to a warmed serving dish. Carve the lamb into cutlets and arrange on top of the couscous. Serve with the yoghurt sauce on the side.

MASCARPONE
— AND —
AMARETTO TRIFLE

Serves 2

250ml/9fl oz milk
25g/¾oz/3 tbsp custard powder
30g/1oz/2½ tbsp sugar
50g/1¾oz/3½ tbsp mascarpone cheese
10 amaretti biscuits/cookies
50ml/2fl oz Amaretto liqueur
1 banana
30g/1oz/¼–½ cup strawberries
125ml/4½fl oz double cream/heavy cream
25g/¾oz/3 tbsp pecan nut halves

Reserve 50ml/2fl oz of the milk in a bowl, and bring the rest to the boil in a small saucepan. Mix the custard powder with the reserved milk and add to the boiling milk, stirring well. Remove from the heat and add the sugar. Allow to cool slightly, then whisk in the mascarpone cheese.

Moisten the amaretti biscuits with the liqueur and place half in the bottom of a serving dish. Peel the banana and cut into slices. Arrange half on the biscuits. Hull and slice the strawberries and arrange half of them on the bananas. Pour on half of the custard. Allow to cool, then repeat with the remaining fruit and custard.

Whip the cream and pipe on top of the custard. Garnish with the pecan nuts.

Opposite: Roasted Rack of Lamb with Figs

Romantic Menu 3

Valentine's Dinner

IN ORDER FOR THIS DINNER TO BE A SUCCESS, THE EMPHASIS MUST BE ON THE DELICACY AND FEMININITY OF THE FOOD, AND, JUST AS IMPORTANT, THE MUSIC HAS TO BE ROMANTIC AND PERSONAL. THE SIMPLE YET FLAVOURSOME STARTER HAS ALL THESE QUALITIES – THE SWEETNESS OF THE BABY PEAS CONTRASTED WITH THE LIME DRESSING BEAUTIFULLY FULFILS ALL THE REQUIREMENTS.

WE CONTINUE IN SIMILAR STYLE WITH THE MAIN DISH OF LIGHTLY GRILLED BRILL SERVED WITH INVIGORATING ASPARAGUS (IT IS CONSIDERED BY MANY AS AN APHRODISIAC) AND A TOMATO DRESSING. TOMATOES WERE ONCE KNOWN AS LOVE APPLES, AND THEY ARE FULL OF VITAMINS, SO IT IS NOT SURPRISING THAT THE SIMPLE TOMATO IS SUCH AN IMPORTANT INGREDIENT IN OUR COOKING. APPARENTLY CASANOVA COULDN'T GET ENOUGH OF THEM!

THE DESSERT FOR THIS MENU IS INCREDIBLY QUICK TO PREPARE AND HAS MAXIMUM VISUAL IMPACT. YOU CAN, OF COURSE, USE OTHER FRUIT SUCH AS BLACKBERRIES, BLUEBERRIES, STRAWBERRIES AND RASPBERRIES, IF YOU PREFER.

MANGETOUT SALAD
❧ WITH ❧
LIME VINEGAR DRESSING

Serves 2

juice of ¼ lime
1 tsp white wine vinegar
pinch of sugar
3 tbsp extra virgin olive oil or grapeseed oil
1½ tsp Dijon mustard
1 tbsp finely chopped shallots
¼ tsp peeled and grated fresh ginger
100g/3½oz small mangetout/snow peas
2 heads chicory/Belgian endive
1 small tomato, blanched, peeled, deseeded and diced
2 tbsp pine nuts, toasted
salt and freshly ground pepper

Mix together the lime juice, white wine vinegar, sugar, oil, mustard, shallots and ginger, and season well with salt and pepper. Set aside.

Blanch the mangetout in boiling salted water for 15 seconds, then drain and refresh in iced water. Dry with a clean tea towel/dish towel.

Remove any damaged outer leaves from the chicory and discard, then take off 14 medium-sized leaves. Wash and reserve them. Cut the remaining chicory in half lengthways, then slice across into 6mm/¼in thick shreds.

Toss the large chicory leaves in some of the dressing and fan out on the serving plates. Toss the shredded chicory, mangetout and diced tomato in the remaining dressing, and adjust the seasoning. Arrange in the centre of the plates and sprinkle with the pine nuts.

GRILLED BRILL
❧ WITH ❧
TOMATO AND HERB DRESSING

Serves 2

8 asparagus spears, trimmed and stalks peeled
2 pieces fillet of brill (or other flatfish such as turbot,
sole or flounder), 150g/5½oz each
1 tbsp vegetable oil
2 tbsp balsamic vinegar
1½ tsp white wine vinegar
3½ tbsp olive oil
2 plum tomatoes, deseeded and diced
1 tbsp chopped fresh herbs (chives, parsley, basil)
a little unsalted butter
salt and freshly ground pepper

Heat the oven to 200°C/400°F/Gas Mark 6. Heat a ridged cast-iron grill pan.

Cook the asparagus in boiling salted water until it is just tender but still firm. Drain and refresh in iced water. Cut each spear in half crossways. Set aside.

Season the pieces of fish and turn in the vegetable oil to coat lightly. Place them on the hot grill pan to mark a criss-cross pattern on both sides. Transfer to a baking pan and finish cooking in the oven for about 7–8 minutes or until the fish is opaque.

In the meantime, mix the balsamic and white wine vinegars with the olive oil in a small saucepan, and season. Warm gently. Add the tomatoes and herbs just before serving.

Reheat the asparagus very gently in a little butter and season.

Place the fish on warmed plates. Spoon over the dressing and garnish with the asparagus.

Opposite: Grilled Brill with Tomato and Herb Dressing

EXOTIC FRUIT GRATINÉE

Serves 2

2 egg yolks
30g/1oz/2½ tbsp caster sugar/superfine sugar
2 tbsp eau-de-vie de framboises (raspberry liqueur)
3 tbsp double cream/heavy cream
½ small mango, peeled and cut into 1cm/½in cubes
½ small papaya, peeled and cut into 1cm/½in cubes
½ kiwi fruit, peeled and cut into 1cm/½in cubes
½ banana, peeled and sliced

Put the egg yolks, sugar and eau-de-vie in a heatproof bowl and set over a pan of simmering water. Whisk until the mixture has trebled in volume, to form a light foamy sabayon. Remove from the pan of simmering water and continue whisking until the sabayon is cold.

Whip the cream lightly until beginning to thicken, then fold into the sabayon.

Heat the grill/broiler to high.

Divide the fruit between 2 individual gratin dishes and spoon over the sabayon to cover. Place under the grill for 1–2 minutes or until golden brown. Serve at once, with ice-cream or sorbet of your choice, if you wish.

Opposite: Exotic Fruit Gratinée

Romantic Menu 4

Ardent Anniversary Dinner

PASSION IS, OF COURSE, INFLAMMATORY AND MUST BE KEPT UNDER CONTROL, OTHERWISE THE FLAMES MIGHT BE BLOWN OUT TOO SWIFTLY. WITH THIS IN MIND, I SUGGEST A LIGHT STARTER THAT LOOKS COLOURFUL AND EATS EASILY, TO BE FOLLOWED BY A RISOTTO WITH A SUCCULENT BABY CHICKEN. TIMING HERE IS CRUCIAL AS THE CHICKEN SHOULD NOT BE COOKED TOO LONG.

FINALLY COMES AN EXTRAVAGANZA OF A BANANA AND GINGER SOUFFLÉ WITH PASSION FRUIT SAUCE. EXQUISITELY LIGHT AND PUFFY, THIS IS INDEED A FINALE TO BE REMEMBERED.

OLD WORLD PRAWN SALAD

Serves 2

125g/4½oz/½ cup cream cheese
2 tbsp crème fraîche
½ small red onion, peeled and finely chopped
2 small celery sticks, diced
1 tbsp chopped fresh chives
50g/1¾oz/½ cup peeled cooked prawns/shrimp,
roughly chopped
1½ tsp lemon juice
1½ tsp white wine vinegar
1½ tbsp extra virgin olive oil
handful mixed salad leaves (radicchio, Little Gem, curly
endive or frisée and lambs' lettuce/corn salad)
10 cooked king prawns or Mediterranean prawns, peeled
salt and freshly ground pepper

Mix the cream cheese with the crème fraîche, then stir in the onion, celery, chives, prawns and lemon juice.

Whisk together the vinegar and olive oil. Toss the salad leaves in this dressing, then season with salt and pepper.

Arrange the dressed leaves in a ring on each serving plate. Place the cheese mixture in the middle and garnish with the large prawns.

Above: Old World Prawn Salad

BONED AND ROASTED BABY CHICKEN
— ON —
RED WINE RISOTTO

Serves 2

2 baby chickens, spatchcocked/butterflied
(split open down the back)
2 tbsp olive oil
½ small onion, peeled and finely chopped
100g/3½oz/7 tbsp risotto rice
200ml/7fl oz red wine
400ml/14fl oz hot chicken stock
25g/¾oz/1½ tbsp unsalted butter
25g/¾oz/¼ cup Parmesan cheese, freshly grated
salt and freshly ground pepper

Heat the oven to 200°C/400°F/Gas Mark 6.

Season the chickens. Heat a little of the olive oil in a heavy-based roasting pan, place the chickens in the pan, skin side down, and transfer to the oven. Roast for 20–25 minutes. Leave until cool enough to handle, then remove the breast bone and rib cage. Keep hot.

While the chicken is roasting, heat the remaining oil in a wide pan and sweat the onion until soft and translucent. Add the risotto rice and stir to coat all the grains with oil. Add the wine, bring to the boil and simmer until almost all the liquid has been absorbed. Add enough chicken stock just to cover the rice and simmer very gently until the rice is just cooked, adding more chicken stock when necessary so that the rice is just covered at all times. The rice should still have a 'bite' to it when cooked, and the liquid should be creamy.

Stir in butter and Parmesan, and season. Place risotto in a warmed serving dish and top with chicken.

Right: Boned and Roasted Baby Chicken

BANANA AND GINGER SOUFFLÉ
❧ WITH ❧
PASSION FRUIT SAUCE

Serves 2

1 tbsp caster sugar/superfine sugar
60g/2oz/¼ cup banana purée (fresh banana
mashed with a fork)
1 tsp cornflour/cornstarch
1 small egg yolk
1 piece stem ginger in syrup, chopped
1 egg white
1 tbsp icing sugar/confectioners' sugar
½ small banana, thinly sliced

For the passion fruit sauce
100ml/3½fl oz passion fruit juice
or fresh passion fruit pulp
½ tsp cornflour/cornstarch

Heat the oven to 220°C/425°F/Gas Mark 7. Butter 2 individual soufflé dishes, each 7½cm/3in in diameter, and coat the sides and bottom with a little of the caster sugar. Set aside.

Put the remaining caster sugar in a saucepan with the banana purée and bring to the boil. Mix ½ teaspoon of the cornflour with a little water and stir into the banana purée to thicken it. Remove from the heat and stir in the egg yolk and ginger.

Whisk the egg white with the remaining cornflour and the icing sugar until the mixture forms stiff peaks. Fold gently into the banana mixture.

Place 3 slices of banana in each soufflé dish, then fill with the banana mixture. Set the dishes in a bain-marie or a roasting pan with water to come halfway up the sides of the dishes. Bake for 20 minutes.

Meanwhile, to make the sauce, mix a little of the passion fruit juice or pulp with the cornflour. Bring the remaining juice or pulp to the boil, then carefully stir in the cornflour mixture. Bring back to the boil, stirring until thickened. Remove from the heat and allow to cool.

Pour the sauce into 2 serving dishes or soup plates. Turn out the soufflés and place one in each dish. Serve immediately.

See Picture on Page 9

Romantic Menu 5

Candlelight Dinner

This calls for a careful selection of music that you know you both like and can relax to. No suggestions from a third party are needed! The food should be a surprise, and full of flavour.

The overture is an elegant courgette flower filled with delicate ricotta, made really gutsy by the olives and a lightly contrasting tuna and caper sauce.

The kick in the main dish comes from the relish served with the prawn and crab cakes.

Incidentally, you can make these cakes with any other fish prepared in exactly the same way.

A surprise comes with the elderflower custard. As with romance and music, every little bit matters, every angle of the relationship must be considered and, above all, the chemistry has to be right! That is what happens with this dessert – the addition of the elderflower has a startling effect and the amount you add is absolutely crucial.

COURGETTE FLOWER
⁂ FILLED WITH ⁂
RICOTTA CHEESE

Serves 2

50g/1¾oz/⅓ cup plain flour/all-purpose flour
¼ tsp baking powder
1 tbsp olive oil
75ml/2½fl oz beer
85g/3oz/⅓ cup ricotta cheese
25g/¾oz/¼ cup Parmesan cheese, freshly grated
1 tbsp chopped black olives
2 courgette flowers/squash flowers
50g/1¾oz/⅓ cup canned tuna in oil, drained
1½ tbsp mayonnaise
1½ tsp lemon juice
½ tsp small capers, washed and drained
oil for deep-frying

Mix together the flour, baking powder, olive oil and beer to make a smooth batter. Leave in a cool place for 1 hour. If there are any lumps, strain through a fine sieve.

Combine the ricotta and Parmesan with the olives. Use to fill the courgette flowers.

Place the tuna, mayonnaise and lemon juice in a food processor and process until smooth. Spread the tuna sauce on the plates and sprinkle with the capers. Set aside.

Dip the flowers in the batter and deep-fry in oil heated to 160°C/325°F until golden brown. Drain on kitchen paper towel, place on the tuna sauce and serve.

Opposite: Courgette Flower filled with Ricotta Cheese

CRAB AND PRAWN CAKES
— ❧ WITH ❧ —
SWEETCORN RELISH

Serves 2

2 eggs, separated

*100g/3½oz/⅔ cup freshly cooked white crab meat, any bits
of shell and cartilage removed*

50g/¾oz/½ cup peeled cooked prawns/shrimp, chopped

2 spring onions/scallions, finely diced

6 cocktail gherkins, finely diced

½ fresh hot red chilli, finely chopped

1½ tsp chopped fresh coriander/cilantro

75g/2¾oz/1½ cups fresh white breadcrumbs

plain flour/all-purpose flour for coating

50ml/2fl oz vegetable oil

15g/½oz/1 tbsp unsalted butter

For the relish

2 tbsp caster sugar/granulated sugar

juice of ½ lemon

1 tbsp red wine vinegar

1 corn-on-the-cob (fresh or frozen)

½ red onion, peeled and finely chopped

½ red sweet pepper, deseeded and finely diced

½ green sweet pepper, deseeded and finely diced

1½ tsp olive oil

salt

freshly ground pepper

Whisk the egg whites until stiff. Fold in the crab meat, prawns, spring onions, gherkins, chilli, coriander and half the breadcrumbs so that the mixture binds together. Season with salt and pepper. Form the mixture into 4 cakes and wrap each one individually in cling film/plastic wrap. Poach or steam for 15–20 minutes or until firm. Leave to cool.

To make the relish, put the sugar, lemon juice and vinegar in a small saucepan. Bring to the boil, then remove from the heat and leave to cool.

Cut the kernels from the corn cobs using a small, sharp knife. Toss the corn, onion and peppers with the olive oil, then stir into the cooled liquid. Season to taste. Set aside.

To finish the crab cakes, lightly beat together the egg yolks. Unwrap the cooled crab cakes and coat them in flour, then in the beaten egg yolks and, finally, in the remaining breadcrumbs. Reshape the cakes if necessary, pressing the breadcrumbs in firmly. Heat the oil and butter in a heavy-based frying pan and cook the crab cakes for 3 minutes or until crisp and golden brown on both sides. Drain on kitchen paper towels and serve with the sweetcorn relish on the side.

Opposite: Crab and Prawn Cakes

ELDERFLOWER CUSTARD
WITH
BERRIES

Serves 2
150ml/5½fl oz milk
4 tbsp elderflower cordial
3 egg yolks
45g/1½oz/¼ cup caster sugar/granulated sugar
200g/7oz/1½–2 cups summer berries (blueberries,
blackberries, raspberries, loganberries, strawberries,
wild strawberries)

Put the milk and cordial in a heavy-based saucepan and bring just to the boil.

In a bowl, cream the egg yolks and sugar together well. Pour on the hot milk mixture, stirring constantly. Pour back into the pan and cook over low heat, stirring with a wooden spoon, until the custard thickens and will coat the back of the spoon. Do not allow the custard to boil. Remove from the heat and pass through a fine sieve.

Place the berries on a plate and offer the warm custard on the side.

Early Morning Surprise

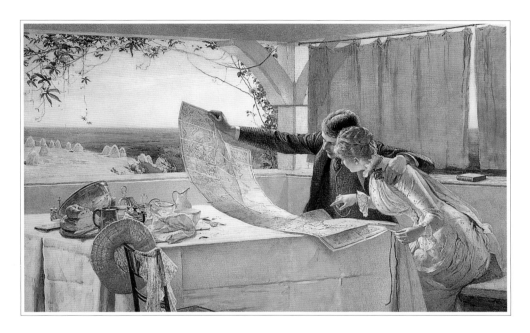

THERE ARE WITHOUT DOUBT VERY FEW PLEASURES IN LIFE SO GREAT AS A BRUNCH IN BEWITCHING COMPANY WITH STIMULATING MUSIC.

I HAVE BEGUN THIS CONCERTO WITH A LIGHT FRUITY STARTER TO AWAKEN THE TASTE BUDS. YOU CAN USE ANY FRUIT, BUT REMEMBER, PRESENTATION IS OF PARAMOUNT IMPORTANCE. IT IS ALL ABOUT FIRST IMPRESSIONS! THEN WE MOVE ON TO THE CLASSIC BRUNCH DISH GIVEN A LITTLE LIFT BY THE ADDITION OF BASIL TO THE HOLLANDAISE SAUCE (FOOD WITHOUT HERBS IS LIKE MUSIC WITHOUT RHYTHM). WITH TOASTED MUFFINS THIS DISH FORMS A WONDERFUL ENSEMBLE OF TEXTURES AND FLAVOURS.

AS BRUNCH IS ALL ABOUT CROSSING BOUNDARIES, WE FINISH WITH WAFFLES MADE MORE EXCITING WITH THE ADDITION OF CARROTS.

FRUITS TO WAKE FOR

Serves 2

½ *papaya, peeled*
½ *mango, peeled*
1 *kiwi fruit, peeled*
½ *small pineapple, peeled*
1 *passion fruit, cut in half*
2 *cape gooseberries*
100g/3½oz/about 1 cup *strawberries, halved*
2 tbsp *icing sugar/confectioners' sugar*
juice of ¼ *lemon*
4 *tips of fresh mint sprigs*

Cut the papaya and mango halves in half lengthways, then cut each piece into a fan. Slice the kiwi crossways, and cut the pineapple into half slices. Arrange all the prepared fruit on the plates with the halved passion fruits. Peel back the papery husks of the cape gooseberries and twist them. Add to the plates.

Place the strawberries, icing sugar and lemon juice in a blender or food processor and process until smooth. Pass through a fine sieve to remove the strawberry seeds.

Pour the strawberry sauce between and around the fruit, and garnish with the mint.

POACHED EGGS ON MUFFINS
⁂ WITH ⁂
BASIL HOLLANDAISE

Serves 2

100ml/3½fl oz *white wine vinegar*
4 *eggs*
2 *English muffins*
4 *slices of cooked ham, cut into rounds*
the same size as the muffins

For the basil hollandaise

1½ tbsp *white wine vinegar*
50ml/2fl oz *dry white wine*
50ml/2fl oz *water*
¼ tsp *white peppercorns, crushed*
1 tsp *finely chopped shallot*
1 tbsp *coarsely chopped fresh basil plus a few stalks*
150g/5½oz/10 tbsp *unsalted butter*
2 *roasted garlic cloves, optional (see Grilled Guinea Fowl*
with Garlic and Herb Crust, page 12)
3 *egg yolks*
Worcestershire sauce
juice of ¼ *lemon, or to taste (optional)*
salt and freshly ground pepper

Bring 1 litre/1¾ pints/1 quart of water and the vinegar to a simmer in a deep saucepan. Crack each egg into a cup, then slide it gently into the simmering water. Cook for about 3 minutes or until all the egg white has set and closed around the yolk. (You might find it easier to cook the eggs one at a time.) Lift the eggs out of the water with a slotted spoon and slide them into a bowl

Opposite: Poached Eggs on Muffins

of cold water – this will stop them cooking and wash off the taste of vinegar. Drain on kitchen paper towels and trim off any straggly bits, then cover and set aside.

To make the hollandaise, place the vinegar, wine, water, peppercorns, shallot and a few basil stalks in a saucepan. Boil until reduced by two-thirds, then leave to cool. Meanwhile, melt the butter slowly, then skim the white sediment from the top. Leave to cool to blood temperature – cool enough to put your finger in comfortably. Squeeze the pulp from the garlic cloves, if using.

Put the egg yolks in the top part of a double boiler or in a heatproof bowl. Pass the vinegar reduction through a fine sieve and add to the egg yolks. Set the pan or bowl over hot water and beat with a whisk until the mixture thickens enough to coat the back of a spoon. Gradually whisk the butter into the egg mixture. Season with salt, pepper and Worcestershire sauce to taste, plus lemon juice, if using. Stir the garlic pulp and chopped basil into the sauce and keep warm.

Heat the grill/broiler to high.

Split the muffins in half and toast them under the grill. Top each with a piece of ham and warm this lightly under the grill.

Put the eggs into a pan of gently simmering salted water just for a minute to heat through, then pat dry with a kitchen cloth and place one on top of each muffin half. Spoon the basil hollandaise over and serve at once.

SWEET CARROT WAFFLES

Makes 5

60g/2oz/4 tbsp butter, softened
1½ tbsp caster sugar/superfine sugar
¼ tsp vanilla seeds scraped from
a split vanilla pod/vanilla bean
2 eggs, separated
pinch of salt
grated zest of ¼ lemon
125ml/4½fl oz milk
125g/4½oz/1 cup less 2 tbsp plain flour/all-purpose flour
100g/3½oz/1 heaped cup carrots, peeled and finely grated
butter or oil for cooking

Put the soft butter, sugar and vanilla seeds into a mixing bowl. Add the egg yolks, salt and lemon zest, and beat with an electric mixer until fluffy. Add half the milk and mix it in, then beat in the flour. Add the remaining milk and stir it in until the batter is smooth. Whisk the egg whites to a medium peak and fold into the batter, followed by the grated carrots.

Heat up a waffle iron and grease the surfaces. Use 2 tbsp of batter per waffle (or more, according to the size of your waffle iron). If you don't have a waffle iron, cook spoonfuls of batter in a heavy-based frying pan to make thick griddle cakes.

Champagne Surprise

W HAT A PRELUDE TO ANY DATE – CHAMPAGNE, SMOKED SALMON AND CAVIAR. THIS REQUIRES SOME SPECIAL MUSIC WHICH REACHES ITS CRESCENDO WITH THE CHOCOLATE PRALINES.

FOR VARIATION, YOU COULD TRY SMOKED HALIBUT INSTEAD OF THE SALMON.

WARM POTATO CROSTINI
❧ WITH ❧
SMOKED SALMON, CRÈME FRAÎCHE AND CAVIAR

Serves 2

250g/9oz/2 cups floury potatoes, peeled, grated and all the liquid squeezed out
3 tbsp vegetable oil
25g/³⁄₄oz/1¹⁄₂ tbsp unsalted butter
120g/4oz smoked salmon, sliced
1 tbsp crème fraîche
2 tsp Ocietra caviar
1¹⁄₂ tbsp olive oil
1¹⁄₂ tsp white wine vinegar
handful salad leaves (such as lambs' lettuce/corn salad, curly endive or frisée, rocket/arugula)
salt and freshly ground pepper

Divide the potatoes in half and season with salt and pepper. Heat half of the butter and oil in a small non-stick pan and add one portion of potato. Press out to a disc about 1cm/¹⁄₂in thick and 9cm/3³⁄₄in wide. Cook until golden brown and very crisp on both sides. Transfer to kitchen paper towel and press gently to remove any excess fat. Keep warm while you make the second crostini with the remaining potato.

Arrange half of the smoked salmon on top of each potato crostini. Add half of the crème fraîche followed by a teaspoon of caviar on each one.

Whisk the olive oil with the white wine vinegar, season and toss the salad leaves in it. Arrange the dressed leaves around the potato crostini and serve immediately.

Left: Warm Potato Crostini

43

CHOCOLATE PRALINES

Makes about 20
a small amount of dry ice (optional)
100g/3½oz/about 1 cup ice-cream of your choice
100g/3½oz white chocolate couverture
100g/3½oz plain dark chocolate couverture

Place a metal tray over the dry ice, if using. Using a small melon ball scoop (Parisian scoop), shape small balls of ice-cream and place on the tray to harden. Stick a cocktail stick/toothpick into each one before it hardens. (If not using dry ice, put the ice-cream balls into the freezer to harden.)

Chop the white chocolate and place in a small heatproof bowl. Chop the plain chocolate and place in another small bowl. Melt both chocolates over a saucepan of simmering water and stir until smooth.

Dip half the ice-cream balls in the dark chocolate, one at a time, and return to the metal tray immediately to harden (in the freezer if not using dry ice). Repeat with the white chocolate. Store the ice-cream balls in the freezer in a rigid container until required. They can be kept frozen for up to a month.

For a dramatic presentation, place a small amount of dry ice in a bowl and pour a little boiling water on to the ice. This forms a 'mist'. Set the pralines on a plate and place on the bowl of dry ice. Serve immediately.

Opposite: Chocolate Pralines

Romantic Menu 8

Alfresco Barbecue

BARBECUES ARE A MELTING POT OF IDEAS, BRINGING TOGETHER DIFFERENT INFLUENCES AND WAYS OF LIVING. THEY MAKE WONDERFULLY FLEXIBLE MEALS IN WHICH YOU CAN RING WHATEVER CHANGES YOU PLEASE.

HERE, TO OPEN THIS SYMPHONY, GRILLED GIANT PRAWNS REALLY COME ALIVE WITH AN AMAZING DRY CARIBBEAN MARINADE. THE SPICE MIX CAN BE USED ON ANY MEAT OR FISH TO BE GRILLED – IT WILL NEVER DISAPPOINT YOU.

TO FOLLOW, A GRILLED SIRLOIN OF BEEF MAKES AN EPIC TEAM ACCOMPANIED BY A RED PEPPER MARMALADE. YOU CAN PREPARE THE MARMALADE IN ADVANCE IF YOU LIKE AS IT WILL KEEP FOR DAYS IN THE FRIDGE. REMEMBER TO TAKE THE MEAT OUT OF THE FRIDGE AT LEAST 1 HOUR BEFORE GRILLING.

WHAT COULD BE SIMPLER OR SWEETER TO FINISH THAN A CHERRY COMPOTE? AND FOR A CHANGE YOU WILL FIND THAT THE SAME TREATMENT IS IDEAL FOR MIRABELLES OR PEACHES.

SKEWERS OF TIGER PRAWNS
❖ IN ❖
SMOKED BACON CARIBBEAN-STYLE

Serves 2

8 raw tiger or king prawns, peeled
8 thin slices smoked streaky bacon
vegetable oil
1½ tbsp olive oil
1 tbsp balsamic vinegar
1½ tbsp white wine vinegar
handful mixed salad leaves of your choice (curly lettuce,
Oakleaf, rocket/arugula, Little Gem, radicchio)
1 tbsp chopped fresh coriander/cilantro

For the Caribbean spice mix
3 tbsp chilli powder
1½ tbsp ground allspice
1½ tbsp ground cumin
1 tsp peeled and finely chopped fresh ginger
½ tsp dried thyme
salt and freshly ground pepper

To make the spice mix, combine all the ingredients. (You'll only need half the quantity, but the rest can be stored in an airtight jar in the refrigerator.)

Wash and dry the prawns. Season with the Caribbean spice mix, rubbing it on to the prawns, then leave to marinate in the fridge for 20 minutes. At the same time, soak 4 wooden skewers in cold water.

Wrap each prawn in a slice of bacon and thread on to the wooden skewers, 2 prawns to each skewer. Turn in a little vegetable oil to coat, then grill over hot coals until the bacon is well coloured and crisp and the prawns are pink, turning to cook evenly.

In the meantime, mix half the olive oil with the balsamic vinegar and the remaining oil with the white wine vinegar. Season both dressings with salt and pepper.

Toss the salad leaves in the white wine vinegar dressing and arrange on 2 plates. Top with the hot prawns and sprinkle with the coriander. Drizzle the balsamic vinegar dressing around and serve.

See Picture on Page 2

GRILLED SIRLOIN OF BEEF
❖ ON ❖
RED PEPPER MARMALADE

Serves 2

1 thick piece of sirloin steak, about 400g/14oz
1 tbsp groundnut oil/peanut oil
15g/½oz/1 tbsp butter
1 sprig fresh rosemary

For the marmalade
2 red sweet peppers
2 tbsp olive oil
½ red onion, peeled and finely chopped
2 garlic cloves, peeled and finely chopped
½ fresh hot red chilli, deseeded and finely diced
½ tsp sugar
1 tbsp red wine vinegar
100ml/3½fl oz chicken stock
1 tomato, deseeded and diced
salt and freshly ground pepper

Heat the grill/broiler to high.

To make the marmalade, grill the peppers until the skin is blistered and well charred on all sides (you can also do this over the hot coals in the barbecue). Place in a plastic bag and leave to cool. When cool enough to handle, pull off the skins, then remove the seeds and ribs. Cut into 1cm/½in squares.

Heat the oil in a pan, add the onion and sweat until soft and translucent. Add the garlic and sweat for a further minute. Add the red peppers, chilli and sugar and sweat for 2 minutes. Add the red wine vinegar and boil until reduced by half. Stir in the stock. Bring to the boil and simmer until very thick. Add the tomato and cook for 3 more minutes, stirring frequently. Remove from the heat and keep warm.

Season the beef with salt and pepper, then turn in the oil to coat lightly. Grill over hot coals for about 5 minutes on each side (for medium-rare). Remove from the heat and leave to rest in a warm place for 1 minute.

Meanwhile, melt the butter in a pan at the side of the barbecue. Add the rosemary and heat gently until the butter is golden brown.

Cut the meat across the grain into 1½cm/⅝in slices. Collect all the juices from the meat and add to the marmalade. Pour the rosemary-infused butter over the beef, and serve with the marmalade.

CHERRY COMPOTE
— WITH —
CLOTTED CREAM

Serves 2

1 small orange
25g/³⁄₄ oz/2 tbsp sugar
100ml/3¹⁄₂fl oz water
150g/5¹⁄₂oz/1¹⁄₂–2 cups ripe sweet cherries, stoned
¹⁄₂ cinnamon stick, cut in half lengthways
1 tbsp Kirsch liqueur
1¹⁄₂ tsp cornflour/cornstarch
2 heaped spoonfuls clotted cream

Pare the zest from the orange in long strips. Put the sugar and water into a saucepan and bring to the boil. Add the cherries, orange zest, cinnamon and Kirsch, and bring back to the boil.

Mix the cornflour to a smooth paste with a little cold water. Stir into the cherry compote and cook, stirring, for a few minutes or until lightly thickened. Remove from the heat and leave to cool, then remove the orange zest and cinnamon stick.

Spoon the compote into bowls and serve with the clotted cream.

Left: Cherry Compote with
Clotted Cream

Romantic Menu 9

Hot Affair

RELATIONSHIPS, MUSIC AND, INDEED, FOOD CAN BE TERRIBLY HOT AND STEAMY AFFAIRS, AND FOR THIS EXCITING OCCASION I WOULD LIKE TO INTRODUCE A TRULY EXOTIC MENU.

FIRST IS A SWEET AND SPICY CRAB SOUP WHICH IS MIXED WITH SOME SWEETCORN TO TAKE AWAY ANY SLIGHTLY AGGRESSIVE EDGE CREATED BY THE HOT CHILLI.

FOR THE MAIN COURSE WE HAVE A DISH OF DUCK BREAST FULL OF CONTRAST – A STRONG MARINADE, AND THE GENTLE SWEETNESS OF A MANGO SAUCE COMBINED WITH THE EXPLOSIVENESS OF BITTERS. THE WHOLE DISH GENERATES JUST ENOUGH HEAT TO TANTALIZE THE TASTE BUDS.

FILO PASTRY IS USED TO MAKE AN EASY VERSION OF THE FAMOUS FRENCH MILLEFEUILLE, BUT MUCH LIGHTER AND HEALTHIER BECAUSE OF THE COMPLETE OMISSION OF CREAM. THIS ALSO ALLOWS THE FULL FLAVOURS OF THE FRUITS TO SHINE THROUGH.

A DIFFICULT CHOICE TO MAKE WHEN IT COMES TO THE MUSIC, BUT I BELIEVE MAHLER'S 'SYMPHONY NO. 5 IN C SHARP MINOR' IS THE PERFECT ACCOMPANIMENT TO THIS HOT AFFAIR.

CREAMED COCONUT, SWEETCORN
AND
CRAB SOUP

Serves 2

1 tbsp vegetable oil
15g/½oz/1 tbsp butter
1 onion, peeled and finely chopped
1 tsp chopped coriander root (or use coriander/cilantro
stalks if root is not available)
1 tsp peeled and chopped fresh ginger
1½ tsp deseeded and chopped fresh hot red chilli
1½ tsp paprika
30g/1oz/3 tbsp canned sweetcorn kernels
300ml/11fl oz chicken stock
50ml/2fl oz canned coconut milk
30g/1oz/¼ cup freshly cooked white crab meat
2 spring onions/scallions, thinly sliced at an angle
salt and freshly ground pepper

Heat the oil and butter in a saucepan, and sweat the onion until soft and translucent. Add the coriander root, ginger and chilli and dust with the paprika. Stir to mix.

Add half the sweetcorn, the chicken stock and coconut milk. Bring to the boil, then reduce the heat and simmer for 10 minutes.

Purée the soup in a blender or food processor, and pass through a sieve back into the pan. Add the remaining sweetcorn, the crab meat and spring onions. Heat through, then adjust the seasoning and serve.

FLO'S DUCK WITH MANGO SAUCE
— AND —
GREEN BANANA RELISH

Serves 2
2 duck breasts
50 ml/2fl oz chicken stock
½ x 400g/14oz can mangoes, drained
dash of Angostura bitters

For the marinade
4 tbsp sweet sherry
1½ tsp Angostura bitters
1½ tsp dark soy sauce
½ onion, peeled and chopped
1 tomato, chopped
1½ tsp dried herbes de Provence
¼ tsp ground ginger
¼ tsp ground cumin
¼ tsp ground coriander

For the green banana relish
1 large green banana (plantain)
1½ tbsp caster sugar/granulated sugar
juice of ½ lemon
1 tbsp red wine vinegar
1 plum tomato, deseeded and diced
½ red onion, peeled and finely chopped
1½ tsp olive oil
½ tsp dried thyme

Combine all the marinade ingredients in a small shallow dish. Score the skin on the duck breasts, cutting into the fat but not into the meat. Add the duck to the dish and turn to coat with the marinade. Turn skin side up, then leave to marinate in the fridge for 12 hours.

To make the relish, steam the plantain in its skin until soft. Peel it. Cut in half lengthways and then across into 2cm/¾in slices. Put into a saucepan. Add the sugar, lemon juice and vinegar. Bring to the boil and simmer until the liquid has evaporated. Add all the remaining ingredients and season with salt and pepper. Remove from the heat and keep hot.

Heat the grill/broiler to high.

Place the duck on a rack in the grill pan (reserve the marinade). Grill for 10–12 minutes, turning over as soon as the skin is crisp. When cooked, leave to rest in a warm place for 10 minutes.

Skim the fat from the juices in the grill pan, then add the reserved marinade and the chicken stock. Bring to the boil quickly and boil to reduce and thicken. Put the mangoes into a food processor with a dash of bitters and blend to a purée. Pour into a saucepan and heat gently. Add the duck juices and stir.

Place the hot green banana relish on the plates. Cut each duck breast diagonally into 6 pieces and place on top of the relish. Pour the sauce around and serve.

Opposite: Flo's Duck with Mango Sauce

EXOTIC FILO LEAVES

Serves 2

6 rounds of filo pastry, each 10cm/4in in diameter
50ml/2fl oz double cream/heavy cream
1 tbsp icing sugar/confectioners' sugar plus more to dust
50ml/2fl oz plain Greek yoghurt/thick plain yoghurt
100g/3½oz/1 cup exotic fruits (mango, papaya, pineapple,
orange, kiwi), peeled and cut into even cubes

For the sauce
100g/3½oz/about 1 cup strawberries, hulled
2 tbsp icing sugar/confectioners' sugar
½ tsp lemon juice

Heat the oven to 200°C/400°F/Gas Mark 6.

Place the filo rounds on 2 greased baking sheets. Brush lightly with water and bake for 10–15 minutes or until golden and lightly puffed up. Leave to cool.

To make the sauce, purée the strawberries with the icing sugar and lemon juice in a blender or food processor. Pass through a fine sieve, and set aside.

Whip the cream with the icing sugar until it forms soft peaks, then stir in the yoghurt. Carefully fold all the fruit into the cream mixture.

Place a filo disc on each plate and spoon a little of the fruit mixture on top. Cover with another filo disc and add the rest of the fruit. Dust a third filo disc with icing sugar and place on top. Pour the sauce around and serve.

Opposite: Exotic
Filo Leaves

Persuasive Lunch

QUAILS' EGGS HAVE ALWAYS BEEN CONSIDERED A DELICACY. IN ROMAN TIMES A SUITOR WOULD OFFER HIS BRIDE QUAILS' EGGS THE NIGHT BEFORE THEIR MARRIAGE, TO ENSURE THAT SHE WOULD BEAR HIM MANY CHILDREN. FOR THE STARTER SALAD HERE, THE EGGS MUST BE JUST SOFTLY COOKED SO THAT THE YOLK WILL MIX WITH THE VINEGAR, CREATING AN INTENSELY PLEASURABLE FLAVOUR.

CHOCOLATE IS RIGHTLY CALLED THE FOOD OF THE GODS. FOR THE AZTECS IT WAS SO PRECIOUS, IT WAS USED AS LEGAL TENDER. THEN CHOCOLATE WAS CONSUMED AS A SAVOURY DRINK, SOMETIMES SPIKED WITH HOT CHILLI. THE USE OF CHOCOLATE IN SAVOURY DISHES HAS BEEN ALMOST FORGOTTEN IN EUROPE, BUT THERE ARE SOME DISHES WHERE IT WORKS EXTREMELY WELL – GAME, ESPECIALLY VENISON, IS PERFECTLY COMPLEMENTED BY A LITTLE CHOCOLATE HIDING IN THE SAUCE.

FINISHING THIS MENU ARE WARM APPLE TARTS. THE STAR-SHAPED EDGING ON THE TARTS MAKES THEM VERY ATTRACTIVE, AND THE CINNAMON SPICING BRINGS A WONDERFUL AROMA.

YOUNG LEEK AND QUAILS' EGG SALAD

Serves 2

10 quails' eggs
*300g/10½oz baby leeks, trimmed and cut on the diagonal
into 5cm/2in lengths*
1½ tsp sherry vinegar
1 tbsp balsamic vinegar
1½ tbsp olive oil
2 plum tomatoes, deseeded and cut into wedges
*15g/½oz Parmesan cheese, cut into shavings with a potato
peeler*
1 tbsp chopped fresh chives
salt and freshly ground pepper

Immerse the quails' eggs in boiling water and cook for 2½ minutes. Drain and refresh in iced water. Carefully remove the shells and set the eggs aside in a saucepan.

Blanch the leeks in boiling salted water until tender but still firm, then drain and pat dry.

Mix the sherry and balsamic vinegars with the olive oil and season. Pour half this dressing on to the eggs and warm gently over the lowest possible heat. Toss the leeks and tomatoes in the remaining dressing and season.

Divide the leeks and tomatoes between 2 serving plates, top with the quails' eggs and sprinkle with the Parmesan cheese shavings and chives.

59

VENISON
⁂ ON ⁂
CHOCOLATE SAUCE

Serves 2

2 pieces of venison fillet/tenderloin cut from the saddle,
150g/5½oz each (ask your butcher
for the bones from the saddle)
3 tbsp vegetable oil
½ red onion, peeled and chopped
1 garlic clove, peeled and chopped
1 small carrot, peeled and chopped
a little thyme and bay leaf
a few black peppercorns
100ml/3½fl oz raspberry vinegar
150ml/5½fl oz red wine
250ml/9fl oz chicken stock
1 tbsp dark bitter chocolate cut into small pieces
30g/1oz wild mushrooms (trumpets, girolles/chanterelles
or oyster mushrooms), well washed and trimmed
salt and freshly ground pepper

Right: Venison on
Chocolate Sauce

Heat the oven to 200°C/400°F/Gas Mark 6.

Trim the venison fillets and remove all the skin. Set the fillets aside. Heat a little of the oil in a small roasting pan in the oven. Add the bones and trimmings and roast until well browned. Set the roasting pan on top of the stove. Reserve 1 tablespoon of the onion and a little of the garlic, and add the rest to the bones. Stir over the heat for 2–3 minutes or until the onion is browned. Add the carrot, thyme, bay leaf, peppercorns, vinegar and red wine, and stir well. Bring to the boil and boil to reduce by two-thirds. Pour into a saucepan.

Add the chicken stock and simmer until reduced by half. Pass through a fine sieve and return to the pan.

Boil to reduce further to about 150ml/5½fl oz. Stir in the chocolate over a gentle heat. Keep the sauce warm, but do not allow it to boil again.

Season the venison with salt and pepper. Heat a little oil in a heavy-based pan and cook the venison until seared and brown on the outside, and pink in the middle. Remove and keep warm.

Add the reserved onion to the pan, with a little more oil if necessary, and sweat until soft and translucent. Add the reserved garlic and sweat for a further minute. Add the mushrooms and season. Toss over the heat.

Place the venison on warmed plates. Pour over the sauce and garnish with the mushrooms.

SIMPLE APPLE TARTS
WITH
CINNAMON CREAM

Serves 2

150g/5½oz puff pastry
beaten egg to glaze
50g/1¾oz/¼ cup sugar
150ml/5½fl oz water
4 cinnamon sticks
50ml/2fl oz crème fraîche
45g/1½oz frangipane
1 dessert apple, peeled, cored and thinly sliced
1½ tbsp apricot jam, warmed and sieved

Roll out the puff pastry on a lightly floured surface until it is about 3mm/⅛in thick. Cut out 2 rounds, each 15½cm/6¼in in diameter. Set them on a baking sheet. Re-roll the pastry trimmings and cut out strips 1cm/½in wide. Brush the edges of the puff pastry rounds with beaten egg and place the strips around the edge. Make cuts in the strips of pastry at 2½cm/1in intervals around the outside edge. Fold the right-hand outside corner of one cut over to the left-hand inside corner of the next cut to form a point and press firmly. Repeat until each pastry has a star-shaped edging. Leave to rest in the refrigerator for 20 minutes.

Heat the oven to 200°C/400°F/Gas Mark 6.

While the pastry is resting, make the cinnamon cream. Dissolve the sugar in the water with the cinnamon sticks, then simmer until reduced to a very thick syrup. Leave to cool, then strain and mix thoroughly with the crème fraîche. Set aside.

Spread the frangipane in the middle of the star-shaped pastries and arrange the apple slices over the top. Bake the tarts for 20 minutes or until the pastry is golden brown and the apple soft. Remove from the oven and brush with warm apricot jam.

Serve warm with the cinnamon cream.

Romantic Menu 11

Late Night Supper

THIS IS A TIME TO BE GENEROUS, AND PERHAPS TO ATTEMPT SOMETHING UNUSUAL AND SLIGHTLY EXOTIC. THE LOBSTER DISH FULFILS THESE CRITERIA – IT IS QUICKLY AND EASILY PREPARED, BUT THE ASIAN INFLUENCES GIVE A VERY INTENSE AND EXOTIC FLAVOUR WHICH SHOULD SUIT THE OCCASION WELL.

TO GUARANTEE A HARMONIOUS FINISH TO THE EVENING WE HAVE MARINATED STRAWBERRIES, MELLOW AND SUBTLE IN FLAVOUR. THEY WILL BE A STEPPING STONE TO MORE EXCITEMENT.

AS FOR THE MUSIC, THERE CAN ONLY BE ONE CHOICE: DEBUSSY'S 'SUITE BERGAMASQUE – CLAIRE DE LUNE'.

CRISP FRIED LOBSTER
⁘ WITH ⁘
SESAME SEED DRESSING

Serves 2
2 lobsters, about 750g/1lb 10oz each
1 carrot, peeled
1 courgette/zucchini
oil for deep-frying
4 large basil leaves
½ tsp sesame seeds, toasted

For the dressing
1 small shallot, peeled and finely chopped
¼ tsp peeled and finely grated fresh ginger
½ small garlic clove, peeled and finely crushed
¼ fresh hot red chilli, deseeded and chopped
2 tbsp soy sauce
¼ tsp sugar
2 tbsp white wine vinegar
4 tbsp toasted sesame oil

For the tempura batter
1 egg
50ml/2fl oz iced water
pinch of bicarbonate of soda/baking soda
30g/1oz/3½ tbsp plain flour/all-purpose flour
salt and freshly ground pepper

Drop the lobsters into a pot of boiling water and boil for 5 minutes, then drain and refresh in iced water. When cool enough to handle, crack open the lobster tails and remove the meat, keeping it in one piece. Take the meat from the claws too. Cut the tail meat into 1cm/½in thick slices. Dry with the claw meat on a kitchen cloth. Cover and keep in a cool place.

To make the dressing, mix together all the ingredients and set aside.

Using a vegetable peeler, pare 'ribbons' lengthways from the carrot and courgette. Blanch in boiling salted water, then drain and refresh in iced water. Dry on a kitchen cloth.

Heat oil for deep-frying to 180°C/350°F.

To make the tempura batter, whisk the egg with the water until pale and foamy. Add the bicarbonate of soda and flour, and whisk in quickly, being careful not to overmix. Dip the lobster pieces in the batter, then deep-fry, in batches, for about 2 minutes or until golden brown. Drain on kitchen paper towels, keeping each batch warm while you fry the remainder.

Dip the basil leaves in the last of the batter and briefly deep-fry these as well.

Gently heat half the dressing in a pan and warm the vegetable ribbons in it. Arrange them on 2 serving plates. Top with the lobster and garnish with the basil leaves. Sprinkle with the toasted sesame seeds and serve with the remaining dressing.

Opposite: Crisp Fried Lobster with Sesame Seed Dressing

Above: Hot Strawberries with Ice-cream

HOT STRAWBERRIES
— WITH —
ICE-CREAM

Serves 2
100g/3½oz/½ cup sugar
100ml/3½fl oz water
½ cinnamon stick
grated zest of ¼ lime
½ vanilla pod/vanilla bean
2 tbsp dry white vermouth
12 medium strawberries, hulled
2 scoops ice-cream of your choice
2 tips of fresh mint sprigs

Combine the sugar and water in a saucepan and add the cinnamon stick, lime zest and vanilla pod. Bring to the boil, then remove from the heat. Add the vermouth and stir, then put in the strawberries. Leave to marinate for 1 hour.

Remove the strawberries with a slotted spoon and divide between 2 soup bowls. Pour the marinating liquid on top, then place a ball of ice-cream on the berries. Garnish with mint and serve immediately.

Romantic Menu 12

Impromptu Picnic

As the well-known song says, anything goes – well, almost anything. Creativity and choice, with flexibility to match, is what you need to bring to this meal. It should be fun and produce an easy-going atmosphere.

Robust and wholesome food, with honest flavours, good textures and natural colours, works best. I have chosen dishes that can be left for some time without spoiling or becoming 'tired' and past their best.

The music has to fit the place and occasion, and my choice would be Mozart's 'Eine Kleine Nachtmusik'.

67

GRILLED VEGETABLE SALAD
❧ WITH ❧
FETA AND CAPERS

Serves 2

1 red sweet pepper
1 yellow sweet pepper
4 pieces of plain focaccia, each 1cm/½in wide
and 8cm/3in long
1 medium-sized courgette/zucchini
2 baby fennel bulbs
50ml/2fl oz olive oil
juice of 1 lemon
1 garlic clove, peeled and crushed
6 canned anchovy fillets, roughly chopped
2 tbsp capers, washed and roughly chopped
100g/3½oz feta cheese, cut into 1cm/½in pieces
fresh basil leaves to garnish
sea salt
salt and freshly ground pepper

Heat the grill/broiler to high.

Grill the peppers until the skin is blistered and well charred on all sides. Place in a plastic bag and leave to cool. When cool enough to handle, pull off the skins, then remove the seeds and ribs. Cut into 1cm/½in wide strips and set aside.

Toast the focaccia under the grill until golden on both sides. Set aside.

Cut the courgette lengthways into 3mm/⅛in thick slices. Sprinkle with sea salt and leave for 20 minutes to drain the bitter juices. Rinse and pat dry.

Carefully slice the fennel bulbs lengthways as thinly as possible, taking care to leave on the roots so the slices do not fall apart.

Heat a ridged cast-iron grill pan or griddle. Grill the courgette and fennel slices on the hot grill pan or griddle until marked on both sides, and tender but firm. Season with salt and pepper.

Mix together the oil, lemon juice and garlic. Toss the grilled peppers, courgettes and fennel in this dressing, together with the anchovies and capers. Place on a serving platter and arrange the feta cheese around the edge. Garnish with basil and the toasted focaccia, and serve.

Opposite: Grilled Vegetable Salad

TORTILLA
❦ WITH ❦
CHORIZO SAUSAGE

Serves 4
4 tbsp olive oil
1 large potato, peeled and cut into 6mm/¼in thick slices
1 onion, peeled and finely chopped
2 garlic cloves, peeled and crushed
1 red sweet pepper, deseeded and finely sliced
6 eggs
1 tbsp chopped parsley
½ chorizo sausage (fully cooked), skinned and sliced
salt and freshly ground pepper

Heat half the olive oil in a 23–25cm/8–9in non-stick frying pan and fry the potato slices for about 10 minutes until softened, turning occasionally. Season with salt and pepper, then remove from the pan. Add half the remaining oil to the pan with the onion and sweat until soft and translucent. Add the garlic and sweat for a further minute. Add the red pepper and cook for 2 more minutes.

Whisk the eggs together in a bowl and season with salt and pepper. Add the red pepper and onion mixture and the parsley.

Heat the remaining oil in the pan and pour in the egg mixture. Stir in the potatoes and chorizo and cook, without browning, until the egg starts to set. Pat the surface level and cook for 1 minute without stirring.

Slide the tortilla on to a baking sheet. Place the frying pan over the top and turn the tortilla back into the pan, cooked side up. Cook the second side for about 3 minutes or until lightly browned.

Slide the tortilla on to a plate and cut into wedges to serve. This dish may be served hot or cold. Enjoy any left-over tortilla the next day.

SUMMER CHICKEN
WITH
BLACK OLIVES AND SULTANAS

Serves 2

1 chicken, about 900g/2lb
2 tbsp olive oil
60g/2oz/½ cup button onions/pearl onions, peeled
30g/1oz/½ cup small button mushrooms,
trimmed and halved if large
2 young carrots, peeled and sliced
1 young leek, white and pale green part only, halved
lengthways and then cut across into 6mm/¼in slices
½ small celery stick, trimmed and thinly sliced
150ml/5½fl oz dry white wine
120ml/4fl oz white wine vinegar
450ml/15fl oz chicken stock
5 sprigs fresh tarragon
10 black olives
30g/1oz/3 tbsp sultanas/golden raisins
salt and freshly ground pepper

Remove all the skin from the chicken, then cut into pieces. Heat a heavy-based pan over moderate heat and add the oil. Season the chicken pieces and fry until lightly coloured all over. Do this in batches, if necessary.

Add the onions, mushrooms, carrots, leek and celery and fry for 1 minute, stirring well. Add the wine, vinegar and enough chicken stock to cover the chicken pieces. Add the tarragon stalks. Bring to the boil, then reduce the heat and simmer very gently for about 20 minutes. When the vegetables are cooked (tender but firm), remove them with a slotted spoon and set aside.

When the chicken is cooked, lift out the pieces and put them in a serving dish with the vegetables. Boil the cooking liquid until reduced by one-quarter, then strain it. Chop the tarragon leaves and stir into the liquid. Season with salt and pepper. Pour the liquid over the chicken and vegetables (there should be enough liquid to cover the chicken completely). Stir in the olives and sultanas. Leave to cool, then taste and adjust the seasoning.

Cover the dish and refrigerate overnight. The cooking liquid will set into a light jelly.

TRADITIONAL FRENCH ORANGE TART

Makes a 20cm/8in tart
180ml/6fl oz orange juice
25g/³⁄₄oz/3 tbsp cornflour/cornstarch
grated zest of 1 orange
160g/5¹⁄₃oz/13 tbsp sugar
4 eggs
3 egg yolks
70g/2¹⁄₃oz/5 tbsp unsalted butter, softened
icing sugar/confectioners' sugar to dust

For the sweet pastry
115g/4oz/8 tbsp unsalted butter
50g/1³⁄₄oz/¹⁄₄ cup caster sugar/superfine sugar
1 small egg, beaten
175g/6oz/1 cup plus 3 tbsp plain flour/all-purpose flour

To make the pastry, cream the butter and sugar together until very pale, using an electric mixer. Slowly beat in the egg. Add the flour with a pinch of salt and mix gently to a smooth paste. Cover the pastry and leave to rest in the refrigerator for at least 1 hour.

Roll out the pastry on a lightly floured surface and use to line a 20cm/8in flan tin. (You will probably not need all the pastry.) Line this with foil or greaseproof paper/wax paper and fill with baking beans. Chill for 20 minutes.

Heat the oven to 200°C/400°F/ Gas Mark 6.

Bake the pastry case for 10 minutes. Remove the foil or paper and beans, and bake for a further 5 minutes or until golden brown. Set aside.

Mix the cornflour with a little orange juice in a small bowl. Put the remaining juice in a heavy-based saucepan with the orange zest and 100g/3½oz/½ cup of the sugar. Add the cornflour mixture, stirring, and bring back to the boil. Whisk the eggs and egg yolks with the remaining sugar until smooth. Add to the orange mixture in the pan and whisk vigorously until smooth again. Bring to the boil, stirring all the time. Remove from the heat and whisk in the soft butter. Pour the mixture into the pastry case and allow to cool completely.

Heat the grill/broiler.

Dust the surface of the tart generously with icing sugar, then caramelize under the grill.

Opposite: Traditional French Orange Tart

Romantic Menu 13

Delicious Daydreams

We all love to daydream and there is nothing nicer to dream about than romance, food and music (not necessarily in that order). This menu will set you off in a nice and pleasurable direction. But care must be taken when choosing both the music and the food.

The salad to start with is a dream in itself, best made during the Jersey potato season. Potatoes that are waxy is what it is all about. The combination of warm potatoes, crème fraîche, chives and caviar is indeed exquisite. Incidentally, I devised this salad when Mrs Gorbachev came to the Savoy for lunch. I was asked to add a little Russian touch to the menu. I thought first of beetroot and cabbage, but then I settled for this. She loved it.

Next there is something light and easy to cook. What could be better than a mixed grill of fish? You can use any fish you like. Just remember that different types of fish have different cooking times as their texture and density are different. There is no need to make a lot of sauce for the fish, as a little will go a long way.

The final curtain is a pear dish with an irresistibly sticky sauce. These flavours will make the dream linger on in your tastebuds.

NEW POTATO SALAD
⊰ WITH ⊱
CRÈME FRAÎCHE AND CAVIAR

Serves 2

300g/10½oz small new potatoes
50ml/2fl oz crème fraîche or sour cream
1 tbsp mayonnaise
1 tbsp chopped fresh chives
25g/¾oz caviar, preferably Ocietra or Sevruga
2 small handfuls lambs' lettuce/corn salad

For the sherry vinaigrette
4 tbsp olive oil
1 tbsp sherry vinegar
salt and freshly ground pepper

First make the vinaigrette by whisking together the oil and vinegar in a bowl. Season to taste with salt and pepper. (This will make more vinaigrette than you need, but it keeps well in a screwtop jar in the refrigerator.)

Wash the potatoes, then put them into a pan of salted water. Bring to the boil and cook for 10–15 minutes or until the potatoes are just tender. Drain. When the potatoes are cool enough to handle, peel them. Cut into 6mm/¼in slices and keep warm.

Combine the crème fraîche, mayonnaise and chives in a bowl. Season with pepper and mix well. Add the potatoes and fold in. Add three-quarters of the caviar and mix very gently with the potatoes, lifting the slices to avoiding breaking the caviar.

Spoon the potato and caviar salad into the centre of the plates and top with the remaining caviar. Toss the lambs' lettuce in 2 teaspoons of the vinaigrette and arrange around the potato and caviar salad. Serve immediately.

MELI MELO OF ATLANTIC FISH
❧ WITH ❧
HERB SALAD

Serves 2
2 king scallops/large sea scallops
2 pieces of hake fillet, 60g/2oz each,
all bones and scales removed
2 red mullet fillets, all bones and scales removed
2 pieces of salmon fillet, 60g/2oz each,
all bones and scales removed
vegetable oil
½ small onion, peeled and finely chopped
¼ tsp black peppercorns
50ml/2fl oz dry white wine
2 tbsp white wine vinegar
50ml/2fl oz chicken stock
2 tbsp double cream/heavy cream
40g/1½oz/3 tbsp chilled butter, cut into cubes

For the herb salad
1½ tsp lime juice
1½ tsp white wine vinegar
1 tbsp olive oil
small handful of yellow curly endive or frisée
small handful of rocket/arugula
fresh basil leaves
fresh chervil sprigs
fresh chives
salt and freshly ground pepper

Heat the oven to 200°C/400°F/Gas Mark 6. Heat a ridged cast-iron grill pan or griddle.

Season all the fish with salt and pepper, and turn it in a little oil. Mark quickly on the grill pan or griddle. Remove to a baking pan and finish cooking in the oven for about 5 minutes. Make sure the fish is not over-cooked.

Meanwhile, place the onion, peppercorns, white wine and white wine vinegar in a small saucepan and boil to reduce by two-thirds. Add the chicken stock and reduce again by two-thirds. Add the cream and simmer until slightly thickened. Strain through a fine sieve and return to the pan. Piece by piece, slowly add the butter, whisking constantly. Season.

For the herb salad, mix the lime juice and white wine vinegar with the olive oil. Toss the leaves and herbs in this dressing.

Place the fish on the plates and pour a little sauce around. Pile the herb salad in the middle and serve.

Opposite: Meli Melo of Atlantic Fish

PEARS
✥ WITH ✥
BUTTERSCOTCH SAUCE

Serves 2

25g/³⁄₄oz/1½ tbsp maple syrup
25g/³⁄₄oz/1½ tbsp golden syrup
25g/³⁄₄oz/2 tbsp brown sugar
50ml/2fl oz double cream/heavy cream
30g/1oz/2 tbsp unsalted butter
2 ripe pears
juice of ½ lemon
15g/½oz/1½ tbsp granulated sugar
vanilla ice-cream to serve
sprigs of fresh mint to decorate

To make the sauce, put the maple syrup, golden syrup and brown sugar in a small saucepan and bring to the boil. Add the cream and half the butter, and bring back to the boil. Remove from the heat and set aside.

Peel the pears and cut each one into 6 wedges, removing the cores. Toss in the lemon juice to prevent discoloration.

Melt the remaining butter in a frying pan, add the pears and sprinkle over the granulated sugar. Cook over moderate heat until the pears are just tender but still firm.

Pour the sauce over the pears and stir together gently. Serve hot, with vanilla ice-cream and decorated with sprigs of mint.

Rekindling the Passion

A COUPLE OF YEARS AGO, IN ORDER TO LOSE SOME WEIGHT, I WENT ON AN OYSTER DIET. I LOST A LOT OF WEIGHT, BUT AS FOR THE APHRODISIAC EFFECT . . . I REALLY CANNOT SAY!

BUT LET'S NOT DESTROY A MYTH. OYSTERS ARE TRULY DELICIOUS. HOWEVER, WHETHER EATEN COOKED OR RAW, I THINK THEY NEED A FLAVOUR CARRIER. IN THIS INSTANCE I HAVE USED RAW OYSTERS WITH HOT AND SPICY ACCOMPANIMENTS.

FOR A LONG TIME IN THIS COUNTRY TUNA WAS ONLY KNOWN AS SOMETHING THAT CAME OUT OF A CAN. THE REASON FOR THIS, I THINK, IS THAT WE OVERCOOKED IT. ALWAYS TREAT TUNA AS YOU WOULD TREAT BEEF – ASK YOUR GUESTS HOW THEY WOULD LIKE IT COOKED. BEST IS MEDIUM RARE (IF SOMEBODY ASKS FOR IT WELL DONE, IGNORE THEM!). THE GUACAMOLE, WHICH COMES FROM MEXICO AND CALIFORNIA, GOES WELL WITH MOST FISH AND POULTRY. IT IS EXTREMELY VERSATILE AND A GOOD THING TO HAVE AS A STANDBY.

THE SMELL OF RIPE PEACHES, FRESHLY PICKED IN THE SUMMER, IS SECOND TO NONE IN THE WORLD OF FRUIT. THE RIESLING AND VANILLA POD FOR POACHING HELP TO INTENSIFY THE PEACH ESSENCE WITHOUT TAKING ANYTHING AWAY FROM THE FINAL PRODUCT. THE MACAROONS AND STRAWBERRY SAUCE ARE A MERE COMPANION ON THE JOURNEY TO HEAVEN.

HOT OYSTERS

Serves 2

12 oysters (ask your fishmonger to open them for you)
2 tbsp red wine vinegar
1 small shallot, peeled and finely chopped
½ tsp crushed black peppercorns
2 tsp finely grated fresh horseradish
1½ tsp tomato ketchup
a little Tabasco sauce
10g/⅓oz pickled Japanese ginger
1½ tsp finely chopped fresh dill

Mix the red wine vinegar with the shallot and crushed peppercorns.

Mix together the horseradish, ketchup and Tabasco.

Serve the oysters on crushed ice, sprinkled with the dill. Eat with the vinegar mix, the horseradish and ketchup, and the Japanese ginger, alternately.

SEARED TUNA STEAK
❖ WITH ❖
GUACAMOLE

Serves 2

2 tuna steaks, about 1½cm/⅝in thick, 140g/5oz each
vegetable oil
50ml/2fl oz well-aged thick balsamic vinegar
(if you cannot obtain the aged thick variety,
use twice as much and boil to reduce it by half)

For the basil oil

1 bunch fresh basil, leaves removed from the stalks
150ml/5½fl oz olive oil

For the guacamole

1 small, ripe avocado
½ garlic clove, peeled and crushed
1 small spring onion/scallion
½ tomato, deseeded and finely chopped
juice of ¼ lemon
a few drops of Tabasco sauce
a pinch of cayenne pepper
½ fresh hot red chilli, finely chopped
salt and freshly ground pepper

First make the basil oil. Blanch the basil leaves in boiling water for 2 seconds, then drain, refresh and pat dry. Put in a blender or food processor with the olive oil and process for half a minute. Turn into a saucepan and leave to simmer gently on the side of the stove for 30 minutes. Strain through muslin and set aside.

Heat the oven to 220°C/425°F/Gas Mark 7. Heat a ridged cast-iron grill pan.

Meanwhile, for the guacamole, peel the avocado, remove the stone and cut the flesh into dice. Mix with the garlic, spring onion, tomato, lemon juice, Tabasco, cayenne pepper and chilli. Season with salt. Cover and set aside.

Season the tuna steaks, turn in oil to coat lightly and grill very quickly on both sides on the hot pan to sear and mark. Transfer to a baking pan and finish cooking in the oven until medium – about 3 minutes.

Spread the guacamole on the plates in a circle. Cut each tuna steak in half at an angle and stand on the guacamole. Mix the basil oil with the balsamic vinegar and drizzle around and over the steaks. Serve immediately.

Opposite: Seared Tuna Steak with Guacamole

POACHED PEACHES
❖ FILLED WITH ❖
MACAROONS

Serves 2

50ml/2fl oz Riesling
120ml/4fl oz water
125g/4½oz/½ cup plus 2 tbsp sugar
½ vanilla pod/vanilla bean, split in half lengthways
grated zest of ½ orange
2 large ripe peaches
60g/2oz macaroons
1 tbsp chopped candied ginger
15g/½oz/1 tbsp unsalted butter, softened
1 tbsp brown sugar
150ml/5½fl oz Strawberry Sauce
(see Exotic Filo Leaves, page 57)
1 tbsp crème fraîche

Combine the Riesling, water, sugar, vanilla pod and orange zest in a saucepan and bring to the boil. Reduce to simmering, then add the peaches and gently poach until they are soft and the skin comes off easily. Drain and peel. Cut the peaches in half and remove the stones. Place on a baking sheet with the cut side up.

Crumble the macaroons in a food processor, then add the candied ginger and butter and mix well. Chill until firm.

Heat the grill/broiler to high.

Roll the macaroon mixture into balls and place in the cavities in the peach halves. Sprinkle with the brown sugar and grill until the sugar has caramelized.

Pour the strawberry sauce on to the plates, place the peaches on it and top with the crème fraîche.

Lovers' Lunch

A LOVERS' LUNCH, LIKE A GOOD NOVEL, SHOULD HAVE A GENTLE INTRODUCTION, A STEAMY AND HOT MAIN CHAPTER AND SOMETHING REFRESHING TO FINISH OFF, INNOVATIVE WITHOUT BEING TOO DEMANDING.

WHAT WE START WITH HERE IS A LARGE SCALLOP, AT LEAST 40G/1½OZ IN WEIGHT, WITH AN UNCOMPLICATED, EASY-TO-PREPARE DRESSING THAT HAS LOTS OF CHARACTER BUT WILL NOT OVERWHELM THE FRAGRANCE OF THE SCALLOP. IT IS TOPPED WITH A DELICATE HERB SALAD, MAKING A LIGHT BEGINNING TO A LUNCH À DEUX.

THIS IS FOLLOWED BY CHICKEN WITH A DIFFERENCE. THE DIFFERENCE IS SWEET POTATO, AS BOTH 'CHIPS' AND MASH, WHICH LIFTS THE CHICKEN UP AND REALLY TRANSFORMS IT INTO AN EXQUISITE AND INTERESTING DISH.

AS FOR THE DESSERT, I WOULD LIKE TO THINK THAT, IN SPITE OF IT BEING THE THIRD COURSE, IT ACTUALLY PLAYS THE FIRST FIDDLE IN THIS CONCERTO. REFRESHING AND SLIGHTLY ACIDIC, IT GIVES THE KIND OF FINISH TO THIS MEAL THAT PREPARES YOU FOR WONDERFUL THINGS TO COME.

ORIENTAL SCALLOPS
❧ IN ❧
THAI DRESSING

Serves 2

1 fresh hot red chilli, finely chopped
2 spring onions/scallions
½ tsp peeled and finely chopped fresh ginger
½ tsp peeled and chopped garlic
2½ tbsp toasted sesame oil
2½ tbsp soy sauce
2 tbsp rice wine vinegar
juice of ¼ lemon
½ tsp toasted sesame seeds
½ tsp chopped fresh coriander/cilantro
¼ tsp palm or granulated sugar
1 tsp vegetable oil
4 large king scallops/sea scallops
small handful herb salad (see recipe for Meli Melo
of Atlantic fish, page 76)
salt and freshly ground pepper

Mix together the chilli, spring onions, ginger, garlic, sesame oil, soy sauce, rice wine vinegar, lemon juice, sesame seeds, coriander and palm sugar.

Heat the oil in a non-stick frying pan. Season the scallops and fry quickly until evenly brown, being careful not to overcook.

Place the scallops on warmed plates. Pour over the dressing and top with the herb salad.

Opposite: Oriental Scallops in Thai Dressing

STEAMY SWEET POTATOES
AND
CHILLI CHICKEN

Serves 2

1 large, long orange-fleshed sweet potato
100g/3½oz/1 cup small broccoli florets
100g/3½oz/1 cup small cauliflower florets
2 chicken breasts, with skin
1 tbsp vegetable oil
½ fresh hot red chilli, finely chopped
1 small spring onion/scallion, finely chopped
1 small garlic clove, peeled and crushed
pinch of ground cumin
pinch of cayenne pepper
a little Tabasco sauce
butter
salt and freshly ground pepper

Steam the sweet potato, in its skin, until it is tender but still firm. Set aside to cool. Blanch the broccoli and cauliflower florets in boiling salted water for 2 minutes. Drain and refresh, then set aside.

Heat the oven to 200°C/400°F/Gas Mark 6. Heat a ridged cast-iron grill pan.

Season the chicken with salt and pepper, turn it in the oil to coat lightly and grill on the hot pan until seared on both sides. Transfer to a baking pan and finish cooking in the oven for about 15 minutes.

Meanwhile, peel the sweet potato and cut as much of it as possible into long 1cm/½in thick sticks like chips or french fries. Mash the ends trimmed from the sweet potato with the back of a fork, then add the chilli, spring onions, garlic, cumin, cayenne pepper and Tabasco.

Heat the sweet potato chips and cauliflower and broccoli florets in a little butter, and season. Arrange in the middle of the plates and top with the chicken breasts. Place the mashed sweet potato mixture on top, and serve.

SUMMER TEASER

Serves 2

juice of 2 limes
75ml/2½fl oz Chablis or other dry white wine
1½ tbsp crème de cassis (blackcurrant liqueur)
30g/1oz/¼ cup icing sugar/confectioners' sugar
1 tsp chopped fresh mint
175g/6oz/1½–2 cups mixed summer berries (strawberries, raspberries, blackberries, wild strawberries, blueberries, loganberries)
sorbet or ice-cream of your choice
fresh mint to decorate

Mix together the lime juice, white wine and crème de cassis. Sift in the icing sugar and whisk well to mix. Stir in the chopped mint. Cover and chill for at least 1 hour.

Rinse the berries and dry them carefully. Divide them between serving dishes, such as 2 small soup plates. Strain the lime mixture and spoon it over the berries.

To shape the sorbet, dip a dessertspoon in hot water, then scrape it across the surface of the sorbet, rolling the sorbet on to the spoon to make a neat shape. Put the sorbet on top of the berries, add a sprig of mint and serve.

Opposite: Steamy Sweet Potatoes and Chilli Chicken

Index

PICTURE ACKNOWLEDGMENTS

Food photographs by Laurie Evans

THE BRIDGEMAN ART LIBRARY, LONDON/NEW YORK:
Front cover: *Francesca da Rimini*, exh. 1837 by William Dyce (1806-64), National Gallery of Scotland, Edinburgh; p1 *Fiammetta Singing, 1879* (oil on canvas) by Marie Spartali Stillman (1844-1927) Private Collection/Julian Hartnoll, London; p3 *Mated* by Frank Stone (1800-1859), York City Art Gallery; p11 *A Visit to his Fiancée* by Emile Loubon (1809-63), Musée des Beaux-Arts, Marseilles/Giraudon; p16 *The Serenade* by John Simmons (fl. 1882-89) City of Bristol Museum & Art Gallery; p20 *Gather ye rosebuds while ye may, 1905* (w/c) by Theodore Blake Wirgman (1848-1925) Bradford Art Galleries & Museums; p26 *The Anniversary, 'I love thee to the level of everyday's most quiet need'* – Elizabeth *Barrett Browning, 1909* (oil on canvas) by Albert Chevallier Tayler (1862-1925), Harris Museum and Art Gallery, Preston; p31 *Nordic Summer Evening, 1899-1900* by Sven Richard Bergh (1858-1919) Goteborgs Konstmuseum, Sweden; p37 *Where Next?* (w/c on paper) by Edward Frederick Brewtnall (1846-1902) Private Collection/Christopher Wood Gallery, London; p41 *The Musical Contest* (Conversation galante dans un Parc L'Amoureux Couronne) by Jean-Honore Fragonard (1732-1806) Wallace Collection; p46 *Conversation Galante* by Nicolas Lancret (1690-1743) Wallace Collection, London; p52 *Woman Between Two Ages* by French School (16th century) Prado, Madrid; p58 *Acme and Septimus, c.1868* (oil on canvas) by Frederic Leighton (1830-96) Ashmolean Museum, Oxford; p63 *Courtship in the Park, 1797* by John Opie (1761-1807), National Trust for Scotland; p67 *The Lovers* by Pal Szinyei Merse (1845-1920) Magyar Nemzeti Galeria, Budapest; p74 *The Rose Bower* by Hans Zatzka (b. 1859), Josef Mensing Gallery, Hamm-Rhynern; p79 *Signor Marsilio and his Wife*, c. 1523 by Lorenzo Lotto (c. 1480-1556) Prado, Madrid; p83 *Lovers in a Café* (panel) by Gotthardt Johann Kuehl (1850-1915), Berko Fine Paintings, Knokke-Zoute.